The Path to... Prosperity:

From Poverty

To Profit

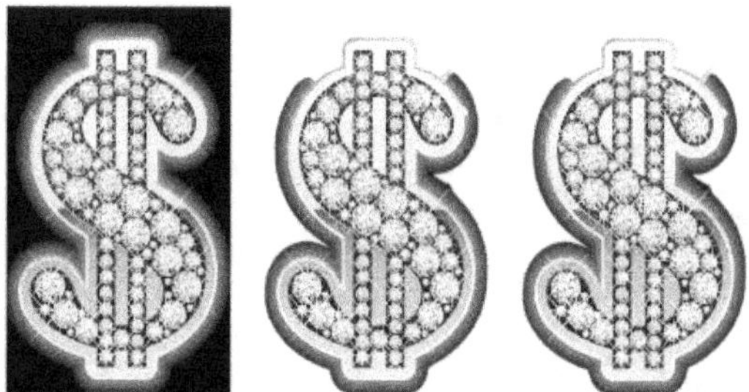

Clyde N. Cook, III

The Path to Prosperity: From Poverty to Profits

 First Edition.

Table Of Contents

Chapter 1: Introduction to Overcoming Poverty

Understanding Poverty: Definition and Causes

Poverty is a complex issue that affects millions of individuals around the world. In this subchapter, we will delve into the definition and causes of poverty, providing valuable insights for anyone wanting to go from poverty to riches.

To begin, let us establish a clear understanding of poverty. Poverty can be defined as a state of deprivation, wherein individuals lack the basic necessities required for a decent standard of living. These necessities include but are not limited to food, shelter, clothing, education, and healthcare. Poverty is not merely a lack of financial resources; it is a multidimensional problem that impacts various aspects of an individual's life.

The causes of poverty are often interconnected and can be categorized into systemic and individual factors. Systemic factors include societal structures, economic policies, and political systems that perpetuate inequality and limit opportunities for upward mobility. On the other hand, individual factors encompass personal circumstances, such as lack of education, limited access to healthcare, unemployment, and low wages.

Understanding the root causes of poverty is crucial for individuals looking to escape its grasp and pursue a path to prosperity. By recognizing the systemic factors at play, one can take steps to challenge and overcome them. This subchapter will explore various strategies and resources available to those in poverty, focusing on niches such as personal finance, entrepreneurship, investing, and real estate opportunities for low-income earners.

For low-income individuals seeking financial empowerment, we will provide practical advice on budgeting, saving, and managing debt. We will also delve into the realm of entrepreneurship, highlighting success stories of individuals from disadvantaged backgrounds who have overcome their circumstances and built thriving businesses. Additionally, we will explore investment options and provide guidance on how to make informed decisions to grow wealth and escape poverty.

Real estate investment opportunities can be particularly attractive for low-income earners, as they offer the potential for long-term financial stability. We will discuss various strategies, such as affordable housing initiatives and government programs, that can support individuals in acquiring property and generating income.

In conclusion, understanding poverty is the first step towards breaking free from its grip and embarking on a path to prosperity. By examining the definition and causes of poverty, individuals from all walks of life can gain valuable insights and knowledge to transform their financial circumstances. Whether you are interested in personal finance, entrepreneurship, investing, or real estate opportunities, this subchapter will provide you with the necessary tools to navigate the journey from poverty to profits and ultimately achieve your financial goals.

The Importance of Financial Literacy

In today's world, financial literacy is more important than ever before. For anyone wanting to go from poverty to riches, understanding the principles of personal finance, entrepreneurship, investing, and real estate is crucial. This subchapter aims to highlight the significance of financial literacy and how it can pave the path to prosperity for individuals from disadvantaged backgrounds.

For those going from poverty to profits, financial literacy is the key that unlocks the door to financial freedom. It empowers individuals to make informed decisions about their money, budget effectively, and save for the future. By equipping themselves with the knowledge and skills necessary to manage their finances, individuals can break the cycle of poverty and create a prosperous future for themselves and their families.

Personal finance for low-income individuals is often a daunting and overwhelming subject. However, through financial literacy, individuals can learn about budgeting, saving, and managing debt. They can gain insights into the importance of emergency funds, retirement planning, and building a strong credit history. Armed with this knowledge, individuals can make wiser financial choices, avoid unnecessary debt, and set themselves on a path to financial stability and success.

Entrepreneurship offers a unique opportunity for individuals from disadvantaged backgrounds to create their own wealth. However, starting a business requires a solid understanding of financial concepts such as cash flow, profit margins, and financial forecasting. By acquiring financial literacy skills, aspiring entrepreneurs can confidently navigate the world of business, make informed decisions, and increase their chances of success.

Investing is another avenue for individuals looking to escape poverty. By understanding the basics of investing, such as diversification, risk management, and long-term planning, individuals can make their money work for them. Investing wisely can provide a passive income stream and build wealth over time, helping individuals break free from the constraints of poverty.

Lastly, real estate investment opportunities can be a game-changer for low-income earners. By developing a deep understanding of real estate markets, financing options, and property valuation, individuals can leverage real estate to generate income and create wealth. Financial literacy is the bridge that allows individuals to seize these opportunities and transform their financial standing.

In conclusion, financial literacy plays a vital role in the journey from poverty to profits. It empowers individuals to take control of their finances, make informed decisions, and seize opportunities for growth. Whether it is personal finance, entrepreneurship, investing, or real estate, financial literacy is the foundation upon which individuals can build a path to prosperity and escape the grip of poverty.

The Power of Mindset: Shifting from Scarcity to Abundance

In the pursuit of prosperity, one of the most critical factors that can make or break your journey is your mindset. It is often said that success begins in the mind, and this is especially true for individuals wanting to go from poverty to riches. In this subchapter, we will explore the power of mindset and how shifting from scarcity to abundance can transform your life and pave the way for financial success.

For those trapped in the cycle of poverty, it is common to have a scarcity mindset. This mindset is characterized by a fear of lack, a belief that there will never be enough, and a constant focus on limitations. However, to break free from poverty and achieve financial abundance, it is essential to cultivate an abundance mindset.

An abundance mindset is characterized by a belief in the limitless possibilities that life offers. It is about focusing on opportunities rather than limitations, and embracing the belief that there is more than enough to go around for everyone. By shifting your mindset from scarcity to abundance, you open yourself up to new possibilities and attract the resources and opportunities needed to succeed.

In this subchapter, we will provide practical strategies to help you shift your mindset towards abundance. We will explore techniques such as positive affirmations, visualization, and gratitude practices that can rewire your brain to think and act in alignment with abundance. We will also delve into the importance of surrounding yourself with like-minded individuals who can support and inspire you on your journey.

Furthermore, we will address the specific challenges faced by low-income individuals in personal finance, entrepreneurship, investing, and real estate. We will provide insights and practical advice tailored to these niches, equipping you with the knowledge and tools needed to overcome obstacles and thrive in these fields.

By adopting an abundance mindset and applying the strategies outlined in this subchapter, you will gradually transform your relationship with money and opportunities. You will begin to see the world through a new lens, one that is abundant in possibilities and ripe with potential for financial growth. Whether you aspire to start your own business, invest in real estate, or simply improve your personal finances, shifting your mindset from scarcity to abundance is the first step towards achieving lasting prosperity.

In conclusion, the power of mindset cannot be underestimated on the path to prosperity. By shifting from scarcity to abundance, you open yourself up to a world of possibilities and pave the way for financial success. With the strategies and insights provided in this subchapter, you will be equipped with the tools needed to transform your life and go from poverty to profits.

Setting Realistic Goals for Financial Success

Achieving financial success is a journey that requires determination, discipline, and a clear vision. For anyone wanting to go from poverty to riches, it is essential to set realistic goals that will pave the way to prosperity. In this subchapter, we will explore the key principles and strategies for setting achievable financial goals that will lead to long-term success.

Going from Poverty to Profits requires a mindset shift and a commitment to transforming your financial situation. The first step in this process is to set specific and measurable goals. Rather than aiming for vague notions of wealth, focus on concrete objectives such as saving a certain amount of money each month, paying off debts, or investing in profitable ventures.

Personal finance for low-income individuals is an important niche that requires tailored strategies. Start by assessing your current financial situation and determining what resources you have at your disposal. Then, set realistic goals that take into account your income, expenses, and financial obligations. It may be challenging at first, but with diligent budgeting, wise spending choices, and seeking additional income streams, you can gradually improve your financial standing.

Entrepreneurship offers a promising avenue for individuals from disadvantaged backgrounds to create wealth. Setting realistic goals in this niche involves identifying a viable business idea, developing a comprehensive business plan, and allocating resources effectively. Consider short-term goals such as launching your business, securing initial customers, and generating steady revenue, as well as long-term goals like expanding your operations and achieving financial independence.

Investing is a powerful tool for escaping poverty and building wealth. However, it requires careful planning and an understanding of the market. Start by setting realistic investment goals, taking into account your risk tolerance, time horizon, and available capital. Consider diversifying your portfolio, seeking guidance from financial advisors, and educating yourself about different investment opportunities to maximize your chances of success.

Real estate investment opportunities can be particularly beneficial for low-income earners. Setting realistic goals in this area involves conducting thorough research, identifying affordable properties, and developing a sound investment strategy. Aim to acquire properties that generate passive income and appreciate in value over time, allowing you to gradually build wealth and escape the cycle of poverty.

In conclusion, setting realistic goals for financial success is crucial for anyone wanting to go from poverty to riches. By setting specific and measurable objectives, tailoring strategies to your unique circumstances, and staying committed to your vision, you can pave the path to prosperity. Remember, the journey may be challenging, but with perseverance and the right mindset, you can achieve financial freedom and transform your life.

Chapter 2: Building a Strong Foundation: Personal Finance Basics

Budgeting: Creating a Plan for Your Money

Introduction:

In the journey from poverty to riches, one of the most crucial skills to develop is budgeting. Creating a plan for your money not only helps you manage your finances effectively but also enables you to pave the way towards prosperity. This subchapter will guide you through the process of budgeting, providing valuable insights and practical tips to help you take control of your financial future.

Understanding the Importance of Budgeting:

Budgeting is the foundation of personal financial success. It allows you to track your income, expenses, debts, and savings effectively. By creating a budget, you gain a clear understanding of your financial situation, enabling you to make informed decisions and set achievable goals. It helps you identify areas where you can reduce expenses, increase savings, and invest wisely.

Creating Your Budget:

To create an effective budget, start by calculating your monthly income from all sources. Next, list all your fixed expenses, such as rent, utilities, and loan repayments. Then, consider your variable expenses, such as groceries, transportation, and entertainment. Categorize each expense and assign a realistic amount to it. Don't forget to set aside funds for savings and emergency funds. This will ensure that you are prepared for unexpected expenses and have a safety net.

Managing Your Budget:

Once you have established your budget, it's important to track your income and expenses regularly. Use tools like spreadsheets, budgeting apps, or traditional pen and paper methods to keep a record of your financial transactions. Review your budget periodically and make adjustments as needed. Stay disciplined and avoid unnecessary spending, focusing on your long-term financial goals.

Making Your Money Work for You:

Budgeting is not just about managing your expenses; it's also about making your money work for you. Explore opportunities for entrepreneurship and real estate investment, even if you come from a disadvantaged background. Seek out resources and programs that provide support and guidance in these areas. Learn about investing in stocks, bonds, and mutual funds to grow your wealth over time. With careful planning and informed decisions, you can turn your limited resources into a path to prosperity.

Conclusion:

In the pursuit of prosperity, budgeting is a vital tool that empowers individuals from all walks of life. By creating a plan for your money, you can take control of your finances, escape poverty, and build a brighter future. Remember, it's not about how much money you earn but how you manage it that determines your success. Start budgeting today and pave your way to financial freedom.

Managing Debt: Strategies for Debt Repayment

Introduction:
In today's society, managing debt has become a crucial skill for anyone wanting to go from poverty to riches. Debt can be a significant obstacle on the path to prosperity, but with the right strategies, it can be overcome. This subchapter aims to provide practical tips and techniques for debt repayment, tailored specifically to individuals from disadvantaged backgrounds, low-income earners, and aspiring entrepreneurs looking to escape poverty and build wealth.

1. Assessing Your Debt:
The first step in managing debt is to assess your current financial situation. Create a comprehensive list of all your debts, including credit card balances, loans, and outstanding bills. Calculate the total amount owed, the interest rates, and minimum monthly payments. This assessment will help you prioritize your debts and develop a repayment plan.

2. Creating a Budget:
Developing a realistic budget is essential for effective debt management. Track your income and expenses, and identify areas where you can cut back to free up extra funds for debt repayment. Allocate a portion of your income specifically towards debt repayment and stick to this budget religiously.

3. Prioritizing Debt Repayment:
It's important to prioritize your debts based on interest rates and outstanding balances. Start by paying off high-interest debts first, as they tend to accrue more interest over time. Make minimum payments on all debts but put extra funds towards the highest interest debt until it is fully paid off. Then, move on to the next highest interest debt and repeat the process.

4. Negotiating with Creditors:
If you find it difficult to meet your debt obligations, reach out to your creditors and explain your situation. Many creditors are willing to negotiate new repayment terms, such as reduced interest rates or flexible payment plans. Taking the initiative to communicate with creditors can alleviate financial stress and make debt repayment more manageable.

5. Consolidating and Refinancing:
Consider consolidating multiple debts into a single loan with a lower interest rate. This can simplify your repayment process and potentially save you money in the long run. Additionally, explore the option of refinancing high-interest loans to reduce monthly payments and interest charges.

Conclusion:
Managing debt is an essential skill for anyone on the path to prosperity. By assessing your debt, creating a budget, prioritizing repayment, negotiating with creditors, and exploring consolidation and refinancing options, you can take control of your financial situation and pave the way towards a debt-free and prosperous future. Remember, with dedication and perseverance, you can overcome debt and achieve your goals of going from poverty to profits.

Saving and Emergency Funds: Creating a Safety Net

In the journey from poverty to riches, one of the crucial steps is to establish a solid financial foundation. This includes building savings and emergency funds to create a safety net that can cushion you during unexpected financial hardships. Whether you are aiming for personal finance stability, entrepreneurship, or real estate investment opportunities, having a safety net in place is essential.

For low-income individuals, saving may seem like an impossible task. However, by adopting a strategic approach and making small changes to your financial habits, you can gradually accumulate savings and create an emergency fund.

Start by setting clear financial goals and envisioning the benefits of having a safety net. Understand that emergencies can happen to anyone, and having funds readily available can prevent you from falling back into poverty. Motivate yourself by reminding yourself of the peace of mind and financial security that comes with having savings.

Begin by tracking your expenses and creating a budget. Identify areas where you can cut back on unnecessary spending and redirect those funds towards savings. Even small amounts can add up over time. Consider automating your savings by setting up automatic transfers from your checking account to a dedicated savings account. This way, you won't be tempted to spend the money before saving it.

Another effective strategy is to create an emergency fund specifically for unexpected expenses. Aim to save at least three to six months' worth of living expenses to provide a safety net during difficult times. This fund should be easily accessible, preferably in a separate savings account, so you're not tempted to dip into it for non-emergency situations.

To accelerate your journey from poverty to profits, consider exploring entrepreneurship or investing opportunities. Having a safety net of savings can provide you with the confidence to take calculated risks and pursue your business or investment ventures.

Remember, building savings and emergency funds is a gradual process. It requires discipline, determination, and a long-term perspective. Stay focused on your financial goals, seek out resources, and surround yourself with a supportive network that can provide guidance and encouragement.

By creating a safety net through savings and emergency funds, you are taking a significant step towards securing your financial future. With time, dedication, and smart financial decisions, you can go from poverty to profits and achieve long-lasting prosperity.

Understanding Credit: Building and Repairing Your Credit Score

In today's world, credit has become an essential tool for financial success. Whether you're looking to buy a car, rent an apartment, start a business, or even apply for a job, your credit score plays a significant role in determining your financial worthiness. Unfortunately, for many individuals from disadvantaged backgrounds, building and repairing their credit score can seem like an insurmountable challenge. But fear not, because in this subchapter, we will unravel the mysteries of credit and equip you with the knowledge and strategies to turn your financial situation around.

To begin with, we will delve into the basics of credit, explaining what it is, how it works, and why it is crucial for your financial well-being. We will demystify terms such as credit score, credit report, and credit history, and show you how these factors impact your ability to access loans, secure housing, and even pursue entrepreneurial endeavors.

Next, we will explore various strategies for building and repairing your credit score. From the establishment of a solid credit history to the responsible utilization of credit cards, we will guide you through the essential steps necessary to improve your financial standing. We will also address the importance of making timely payments, managing your debt-to-income ratio, and how to dispute any errors or inaccuracies on your credit report.

Moreover, we will provide practical advice on how to rebuild your credit score if it has been damaged due to past financial hardships. We will discuss the benefits of secured credit cards, credit-builder loans, and the power of consistent and responsible financial habits.

Throughout this subchapter, we will emphasize the importance of financial literacy and education. We understand that the path from poverty to profits can be filled with obstacles and setbacks. Therefore, we will provide you with valuable resources and recommend financial education programs that can further assist you on your journey towards financial independence.

By understanding credit and implementing the strategies presented in this subchapter, you will be well-equipped to build and repair your credit score. This newfound knowledge will not only help you secure loans and financial opportunities but also empower you to take control of your financial future. Remember, with determination, perseverance, and the right tools, you can transcend poverty and achieve prosperity.

So, let's embark on this transformative journey together and unlock the doors to financial success.

Chapter 3: Entrepreneurship as a Path to Prosperity

Identifying Your Passions and Skills

Subchapter: Identifying Your Passions and Skills

Introduction:
In order to embark on the path to prosperity, it is crucial to identify your passions and skills. This subchapter will guide you through the process of discovering your unique talents and interests, and how to leverage them to break free from poverty and achieve financial success. Whether you are looking to start your own business, invest in real estate, or improve your personal finances, understanding your passions and skills will be the foundation for your journey towards prosperity.

Identifying Your Passions:
Passions are the fuel that ignites our drive and enthusiasm. They are the activities that bring us joy, fulfillment, and a sense of purpose. To identify your passions, take some time for self-reflection. Consider the activities or hobbies that make you lose track of time, the subjects you find yourself naturally drawn to, and the causes that resonate with you. These clues will lead you to your true passions and provide direction for your path to prosperity.

Discovering Your Skills:
Skills are the practical abilities and knowledge that we possess. They are the tools we can use to make a living and excel in our chosen fields. To uncover your skills, evaluate your past experiences, both personal and professional. What have you excelled at? What tasks come easily to you? What have others praised you for? Additionally, consider any formal education, certifications, or specialized training you have received. Identifying your skills will help you leverage them to create opportunities for financial growth and success.

Aligning Passions and Skills:
Once you have identified your passions and skills, the next step is to align them. This synergy will enable you to pursue a career or business that brings you both joy and financial rewards. Look for ways to incorporate your passions into your work by exploring industries, professions, or entrepreneurial ventures that align with your interests. Additionally, seek opportunities to enhance your skills through further education, training, or mentorship programs. The more you can align your passions and skills, the greater your chances of achieving prosperity.

Conclusion:
Identifying your passions and skills is a crucial step on the path from poverty to profits. By understanding what truly inspires you and recognizing your unique abilities, you can unlock opportunities for success and financial freedom. Whether you choose entrepreneurship, real estate investment, personal finance management, or any other avenue, embracing your passions and leveraging your skills will empower you to overcome adversity and create a prosperous future.

Overcoming Barriers: Navigating Challenges as an Entrepreneur

In the journey from poverty to profits, the path is never smooth. As an aspiring entrepreneur, you are likely to face numerous barriers and challenges along the way. However, it's essential to understand that these obstacles can be overcome with determination, resilience, and the right mindset. In this subchapter, we will explore the various barriers you may encounter and provide strategies to navigate them successfully.

One of the primary barriers you may face is a lack of resources and financial capital. As someone coming from a low-income background, it can be daunting to start a business without access to traditional funding sources. However, don't let this discourage you. There are alternative financing options available such as microloans, crowdfunding, or seeking out grants and subsidies specifically designed for individuals from disadvantaged backgrounds. Additionally, focusing on bootstrapping your business and seeking partnerships can help alleviate financial limitations.

Another significant hurdle may be a lack of knowledge and skills. As an entrepreneur, continuous learning is crucial. Seek out educational resources, attend workshops, and network with mentors who can guide you through the process. Embrace the mindset of a lifelong learner and don't be afraid to ask for help. Remember, knowledge is power, and acquiring new skills will enable you to navigate challenges more effectively.

Moreover, societal and cultural biases can pose significant barriers for individuals from disadvantaged backgrounds. It's crucial to develop a strong support network, surround yourself with like-minded individuals who believe in your potential, and seek out mentors who have successfully overcome similar challenges. Remember, your background does not define your future; it's your determination and perseverance that will lead you to success.

Another obstacle you may encounter is the fear of failure. Understand that failure is a part of the entrepreneurial journey. Embrace it as a learning opportunity and use it to fuel your motivation. Develop resilience and learn from your mistakes. Remember that many successful entrepreneurs faced multiple failures before achieving their goals.

In conclusion, the path from poverty to profits is filled with obstacles. However, with the right mindset, determination, and a willingness to learn, you can overcome these barriers. Embrace the challenges as opportunities for growth, seek out resources and support, and never give up on your dreams. By navigating these challenges successfully, you will pave the way towards a prosperous future as an entrepreneur.

Business Planning: Developing a Solid Business Model

In the journey from poverty to profits, one crucial step is to develop a solid business model that will pave the way to financial prosperity. A business model serves as the blueprint for your enterprise, outlining how you will generate revenue, create value, and achieve sustainable success. This subchapter aims to guide anyone wanting to go from poverty to riches, specifically those interested in going from poverty to profits, personal finance for low-income individuals, entrepreneurship for individuals from disadvantaged backgrounds, investing for individuals looking to escape poverty, and real estate investment opportunities for low-income earners.

Starting with the basics, this subchapter will cover the importance of a business plan and how it acts as a roadmap for your entrepreneurial journey. We will delve into the key elements of a business model, including identifying your target market, understanding your value proposition, and determining your revenue streams. By providing actionable steps and practical examples, we will help individuals develop a comprehensive and tailored business plan that aligns with their specific goals and circumstances.

Furthermore, we will address the challenges faced by low-income individuals when it comes to business planning and offer strategies to overcome them. We believe that everyone, regardless of their background or financial situation, can become a successful entrepreneur with the right guidance and support. We will share inspiring success stories of individuals who have triumphed over adversity, proving that poverty should never be a barrier to achieving financial independence.

For those interested in investing and real estate opportunities, this subchapter will explore different investment avenues suitable for low-income earners. We will provide insights into how to identify lucrative investment options, secure financing, and leverage resources effectively. Through practical tips and expert advice, readers will gain the knowledge and confidence to embark on their investment journey and create wealth for themselves and their communities.

Whether you have a business idea in mind or are simply seeking ways to improve your financial situation, this subchapter will provide valuable insights and tools to develop a solid business model. By empowering individuals to take control of their financial destiny, we hope to inspire a new wave of entrepreneurs who will not only escape poverty but also create positive change in their lives and communities. Together, let us embark on the path to prosperity and turn dreams of riches into a reality.

Marketing and Sales: Reaching Your Target Audience

In today's competitive and ever-changing world, marketing and sales play a vital role in the success of any business. Whether you are an aspiring entrepreneur, a low-income individual looking to improve your personal finance, or someone seeking to escape poverty through investments or real estate, understanding how to reach your target audience is crucial on your path to prosperity.

Marketing is the process of promoting and selling products or services to customers. It involves identifying your target audience, understanding their needs and wants, and creating strategies to reach and engage them effectively. Sales, on the other hand, is the act of converting potential customers into actual buyers. Together, marketing and sales form the backbone of any successful business venture.

For individuals aiming to go from poverty to profits, marketing and sales can be powerful tools to create financial stability and long-term wealth. By identifying your target audience, you can tailor your products or services to meet their specific needs. For example, if you are an entrepreneur from a disadvantaged background, you may have unique insights into the challenges faced by individuals in similar circumstances. By leveraging this knowledge, you can develop products or services that address these challenges and provide value to your target audience.

To effectively reach your target audience, it is essential to utilize various marketing channels and strategies. In today's digital age, social media platforms, websites, and online advertising can be highly effective in reaching a wide audience. However, traditional marketing methods such as print media, networking events, and community engagement should not be overlooked, as they can provide valuable opportunities to connect with your target audience on a more personal level.

In addition to marketing, mastering the art of sales is crucial for individuals looking to escape poverty through investments or real estate. Selling requires effective communication skills, negotiation abilities, and a deep understanding of your product or service. By honing these skills, you can confidently present your investment opportunities or real estate ventures to potential buyers or investors, increasing your chances of success.

In conclusion, marketing and sales are essential components on your path to prosperity. By understanding your target audience, tailoring your products or services to meet their needs, and effectively reaching them through various marketing channels, you can significantly improve your chances of going from poverty to profits. Whether you are focused on personal finance, entrepreneurship, investments, or real estate, mastering these skills will undoubtedly contribute to your journey towards financial stability and long-term wealth.

Chapter 4: Investing for Financial Growth

Investment Basics: Understanding Different Asset Classes

If you are someone who desires to go from poverty to riches, it is essential to grasp the fundamentals of investing. In this subchapter, we will delve into the world of investment basics, specifically focusing on understanding different asset classes. By acquiring this knowledge, you will be equipped with the necessary tools to make informed investment decisions and pave your path to prosperity.

Asset classes refer to various types of investments that individuals can choose from to grow their wealth. Each asset class possesses its own unique characteristics, risk levels, and potential returns. By diversifying your portfolio across different asset classes, you can mitigate risk and maximize your earning potential.

The four primary asset classes are stocks, bonds, real estate, and commodities. Stocks represent ownership in a company and offer the potential for capital appreciation and dividends. Bonds, on the other hand, are debt securities issued by governments or corporations, providing fixed interest payments over a specified period.

Real estate investment opportunities can be incredibly lucrative, especially for low-income earners. This asset class includes residential, commercial, and industrial properties that can appreciate in value and generate rental income. Real estate also serves as a hedge against inflation, making it an attractive investment option.

Commodities encompass tangible goods such as gold, oil, natural gas, and agricultural products. Investing in commodities can act as a hedge against inflation and diversify your portfolio. However, it is important to be aware of the unique risks associated with this asset class, such as price volatility and geopolitical factors.

Understanding the characteristics and potential risks of each asset class is crucial for making informed investment decisions. By aligning your investment choices with your financial goals and risk tolerance, you can optimize your chances of escaping poverty and achieving long-term prosperity.

Moreover, it is essential to note that investments should be tailored to your unique circumstances and financial capabilities. As someone from a low-income background, you may need to approach investing with a different perspective and focus on strategies that are suitable for your situation.

In the upcoming chapters, we will explore specific investment strategies and tactics that are tailored to low-income individuals and entrepreneurs from disadvantaged backgrounds. By combining the knowledge of different asset classes with practical investment techniques, you will be well on your way to transforming your financial situation and unlocking the path to prosperity.

Creating a Diversified Investment Portfolio

In the journey from poverty to riches, one crucial step is to create a diversified investment portfolio. This subchapter aims to guide individuals from disadvantaged backgrounds, low-income earners, and those looking to escape poverty on how to build a solid foundation for financial success through investing.

Investing can be intimidating, especially for individuals with limited financial resources. However, it is essential to understand that investing is not reserved for the wealthy alone. By adopting a strategic approach and making informed decisions, anyone can begin their path to prosperity.

Diversification is a key principle that mitigates risk and maximizes returns. Instead of putting all your eggs in one basket, a diversified portfolio spreads investments across various asset classes such as stocks, bonds, real estate, and alternative investments. By doing so, you minimize the impact of one investment's poor performance on your overall portfolio.

For those with limited funds, it is crucial to start small and gradually build your portfolio. Begin by setting aside a portion of your income for investing purposes. Even a small amount regularly invested can yield significant returns over time. Consider low-cost index funds or exchange-traded funds (ETFs) as a starting point, as they offer broad market exposure at a minimal cost.

Real estate investment presents a unique opportunity for low-income earners. Look for affordable properties in up-and-coming areas or explore options like real estate investment trusts (REITs) that allow you to invest in real estate without the need for substantial capital. Real estate has the potential for long-term growth and can provide a steady stream of passive income.

Entrepreneurship is another avenue to consider. By starting your own business, you can control your financial destiny and generate wealth. Look for opportunities in your community or leverage your skills and talents to create a product or service that meets market demand. Focus on creating a strong business plan, seeking mentorship, and accessing resources available to entrepreneurs from disadvantaged backgrounds.

Lastly, as you embark on your journey to financial prosperity, it is crucial to educate yourself continuously. Stay informed about market trends, investment strategies, and personal finance principles. Attend workshops, read books, and engage with online communities to expand your knowledge.

Remember, building wealth takes time and patience. Be prepared for setbacks and learn from your mistakes. By creating a diversified investment portfolio, exploring real estate opportunities, considering entrepreneurship, and continuously educating yourself, you are taking significant steps towards escaping poverty and achieving financial prosperity.

Risk Management: Protecting Your Investments

In the journey from poverty to riches, one crucial aspect that cannot be overlooked is risk management. When it comes to investing, protecting your hard-earned money becomes paramount. This subchapter aims to equip individuals from all walks of life with the necessary knowledge and strategies to safeguard their investments and increase their chances of financial success.

For those on the path from poverty to profits, personal finance is a key area to focus on. By understanding the principles of budgeting, saving, and investing, individuals can escape the cycle of poverty and achieve financial independence. However, this journey is not without risks. That's where risk management steps in.

Entrepreneurship offers a way out of poverty for many individuals from disadvantaged backgrounds. Starting a business can be both rewarding and risky. By implementing effective risk management techniques, such as diversifying revenue streams, conducting market research, and creating contingency plans, entrepreneurs can protect their investments and increase their chances of long-term success.

Investing is another avenue individuals can explore to escape poverty. However, the world of investing can be complex and unpredictable. It is essential to understand the risks associated with different investment options and develop a risk management strategy. This subchapter will provide insights into various investment opportunities suitable for low-income earners and offer practical advice on minimizing risks.

Real estate investment presents a unique opportunity for low-income earners to build wealth. However, it is not without its risks. This subchapter will delve into the world of real estate investment, highlighting the potential benefits and risks involved. From understanding market trends to conducting due diligence, readers will gain valuable insights into risk management strategies specific to real estate investments.

Ultimately, risk management is about protecting your investments and minimizing potential losses. This subchapter will provide practical tips and advice on diversification, asset allocation, setting realistic expectations, and developing an emergency fund. By implementing these risk management strategies, individuals on the path to prosperity can navigate the financial landscape with confidence and increase their chances of achieving long-term financial success.

In conclusion, this subchapter on risk management aims to empower individuals looking to escape poverty by equipping them with the necessary tools and knowledge to protect their investments. By understanding and implementing effective risk management strategies, readers can pave the way for a brighter financial future and move closer to their goal of achieving prosperity.

Long-Term Investing Strategies for Wealth Accumulation

Introduction

In this subchapter, we will explore long-term investing strategies that can help individuals go from poverty to riches. Whether you are someone who dreams of escaping poverty, seeking personal finance solutions on a limited income, aspiring to become an entrepreneur from a disadvantaged background, or looking for opportunities to invest and build wealth, this chapter will provide valuable insights and guidance.

1. The Power of Compound Interest

One of the most fundamental principles of wealth accumulation is harnessing the power of compound interest. By consistently investing even small amounts of money over a long period, you can benefit from the compounding effect and see your wealth grow significantly. We will delve into various investment vehicles that can help you leverage compound interest to your advantage.

2. Diversification and Risk Management

Another crucial aspect of long-term investing is diversification. We will discuss the importance of spreading your investments across different asset classes, such as stocks, bonds, real estate, and mutual funds. By diversifying your portfolio, you can mitigate risks and increase the potential for long-term wealth accumulation.

3. Building a Strong Investment Portfolio

We will explore different investment strategies tailored to low-income individuals. From starting with small amounts in index funds or exchange-traded funds (ETFs) to leveraging tax-efficient investment accounts like Roth IRAs, we will provide practical advice on building a strong investment portfolio even with limited resources.

4. Real Estate Investment Opportunities

Real estate can be a lucrative investment avenue, especially for low-income earners. We will discuss various real estate investment opportunities, such as rental properties, house flipping, and real estate investment trusts (REITs). We will also cover financing options and strategies for those with limited access to traditional bank loans.

5. Entrepreneurial Ventures and Wealth Creation

For individuals from disadvantaged backgrounds, entrepreneurship can be a path to prosperity. We will explore the mindset, skills, and resources necessary to embark on entrepreneurial ventures. Additionally, we will discuss strategies to invest the profits generated from your entrepreneurial endeavors to further accumulate wealth.

Conclusion

Long-term investing is a powerful tool for wealth accumulation. By understanding the principles of compound interest, diversification, and risk management, low-income individuals can build a strong investment portfolio and escape poverty. Additionally, we will explore specific opportunities in real estate investment and entrepreneurship, providing practical insights and guidance. With the right strategies and determination, you can transform your financial situation and embark on the path to prosperity.

Chapter 5: Real Estate Investment Opportunities for Low-Income Earners

Introduction to Real Estate Investment: Why it's a Viable Option

For anyone wanting to go from poverty to riches, exploring various investment options is crucial. One avenue that holds immense potential is real estate investment. In this subchapter, we will delve into why real estate investment is a viable option for individuals from disadvantaged backgrounds who are looking to escape poverty and achieve financial prosperity.

Real estate investment has proven to be a powerful wealth-building tool, offering numerous benefits that make it particularly attractive for low-income earners. Unlike other investment options that may require substantial initial capital, real estate allows individuals to start with modest investments and gradually build their portfolio over time. This makes it accessible to those with limited financial resources but a strong desire to improve their circumstances.

One of the key advantages of real estate investment is its ability to generate a steady source of passive income. By purchasing properties and renting them out, individuals can create a reliable stream of cash flow that can help cover expenses and build wealth over time. This is especially beneficial for low-income individuals who may have limited employment opportunities or unstable income streams.

Furthermore, real estate investment provides a hedge against inflation. As the value of properties tends to appreciate over time, investors can benefit from capital appreciation and potentially sell their assets at a higher price in the future. This can lead to substantial profits and wealth accumulation, offering a way out of poverty and towards financial freedom.

Real estate investment also offers tax advantages that can significantly impact an individual's financial situation. Expenses related to property management, repairs, and mortgage interest can often be deducted from the taxable income, reducing the overall tax burden. This allows individuals to retain more of their earnings and reinvest them back into their real estate portfolio, accelerating their path to prosperity.

Lastly, real estate investment provides a tangible asset that can be leveraged for further financial growth. Properties can serve as collateral for obtaining loans or lines of credit, enabling individuals to expand their investment portfolio and explore additional avenues for wealth creation.

In conclusion, real estate investment presents a viable opportunity for low-income earners to escape poverty and achieve financial prosperity. Its accessibility, potential for passive income, ability to hedge against inflation, tax advantages, and the possibility for leveraging assets make it an attractive option for anyone wanting to go from poverty to riches. By embarking on a journey into real estate investment, individuals from disadvantaged backgrounds can take control of their financial future and pave their path to prosperity.

Financing Options for Real Estate Investment

When it comes to real estate investment, finding the right financing options can be a crucial step towards achieving financial prosperity. In this subchapter, we will explore various financing options that can help individuals from disadvantaged backgrounds go from poverty to profits through real estate investment.

For low-income individuals looking to venture into the world of entrepreneurship and real estate, it is important to understand that there are several financing options available that can make their dreams a reality.

One option is to explore government-backed loans and grants specifically designed to support low-income individuals. These programs often offer favorable terms, low-interest rates, and flexible repayment options, making it easier for individuals to secure financing for their real estate investments.

Another financing option to consider is crowdfunding. This innovative approach allows individuals to raise funds from a large pool of investors who are interested in real estate projects. Crowdfunding platforms provide opportunities for low-income earners to invest in real estate with smaller amounts of capital, enabling them to diversify their investment portfolio and build wealth over time.

Furthermore, partnerships and joint ventures can be an effective way to finance real estate investments. By teaming up with experienced investors or individuals from similar backgrounds, low-income earners can pool their financial resources and expertise to acquire properties and share the profits. This collaborative approach not only reduces the financial burden but also provides a valuable opportunity to learn from experienced investors.

Additionally, private lenders can be a viable financing option for real estate investment. These lenders are often more flexible than traditional banks and may be more willing to work with individuals from disadvantaged backgrounds. However, it is crucial to thoroughly research and evaluate potential lenders to ensure that the terms and conditions are fair and favorable.

Lastly, cultivating a strong credit score and maintaining good financial habits are essential for accessing traditional financing options. By diligently paying bills on time, reducing debt, and building a positive credit history, individuals can enhance their chances of securing loans from banks and other financial institutions.

In conclusion, financing options for real estate investment are available for individuals from all walks of life, including those from disadvantaged backgrounds. By exploring government programs, crowdfunding, partnerships, private lenders, and traditional financing options, low-income earners can embark on a path to prosperity through real estate investment. With the right mindset, determination, and access to the right financing tools, anyone can turn their dreams of escaping poverty into profitable realities.

Identifying Profitable Real Estate Opportunities

In the journey from poverty to riches, one of the most effective paths to financial success is through real estate investment. Real estate offers low-income individuals the opportunity to build wealth and escape the cycle of poverty. This subchapter will guide you through the process of identifying profitable real estate opportunities, even if you come from a disadvantaged background.

1. Understanding your financial situation: Before diving into real estate, it's crucial to assess your current financial situation. Evaluate your income, expenses, and credit score. By understanding your financial constraints, you can determine the type of real estate investment that suits your budget and risk tolerance.

2. Researching local markets: Real estate opportunities vary from one location to another. Research your local market to identify neighborhoods that are experiencing growth and have the potential for increased property value. Look for areas with amenities, infrastructure development, and a strong job market. Analyze recent sales data and rental rates to determine the profitability of potential investments.

3. Networking and building relationships: Building a strong network is essential in real estate. Attend local real estate events, join investor groups, and connect with professionals in the industry. By networking, you can gain valuable insights, find potential partners or mentors, and access off-market deals that are not available to the general public.

4. Utilizing creative financing options: Low-income earners often face challenges when it comes to securing financing for real estate investments. However, there are various creative financing options available, such as government-backed loans, private lenders, or partnerships with more experienced investors. Explore these options to overcome financial barriers and capitalize on profitable opportunities.

5. Analyzing risk and return: Real estate investments come with risks, and it's crucial to assess and manage them effectively. Conduct thorough due diligence on potential properties, including physical inspections, title searches, and financial analysis. Evaluate the potential return on investment, factoring in expenses, potential appreciation, and rental income.

6. Diversifying your portfolio: As you progress on your path to prosperity, consider diversifying your real estate portfolio. Explore different types of properties, such as residential, commercial, or multi-family units. Diversification helps spread risk and increases the potential for higher returns.

Remember, real estate investment is a journey that requires continuous learning and adaptation. Stay up-to-date with market trends, regulations, and investment strategies. Embrace the entrepreneurial mindset and be prepared to take calculated risks. With determination, perseverance, and the knowledge gained from this subchapter, you can identify profitable real estate opportunities and pave your way from poverty to profits.

Rental Property Management: Maximizing Returns on Investment

For anyone wanting to go from poverty to riches, understanding the power of real estate investment is crucial. In this subchapter, we will explore the world of rental property management and how it can help individuals maximize their returns on investment, paving the way to prosperity.

Personal finance for low-income individuals often involves finding creative ways to generate passive income. Real estate investment offers an opportunity for individuals from disadvantaged backgrounds to break free from the chains of poverty. By owning and managing rental properties, one can build a steady stream of income that can significantly improve their financial situation.

Entrepreneurship is a path that many individuals from disadvantaged backgrounds choose to escape poverty. By venturing into real estate investment, aspiring entrepreneurs can leverage their properties to generate wealth. However, success in this field heavily relies on effective property management. This subchapter will provide key insights and strategies to help these individuals navigate the complex world of rental property management.

Investing for individuals looking to escape poverty requires careful consideration and planning. Real estate investment offers a unique opportunity to build long-term wealth, but it also comes with risks. This subchapter will delve into the essential elements of rental property management, such as tenant screening, property maintenance, and financial management. By mastering these skills, individuals can ensure their investments remain profitable and secure their path to prosperity.

Real estate investment opportunities for low-income earners may seem daunting at first, but with the right knowledge and resources, it can be a transformative endeavor. This subchapter will provide practical advice on finding affordable properties, securing financing, and managing rental properties on a limited budget. It will also explore alternative options such as investing in real estate investment trusts (REITs) or partnering with other investors, making the path to real estate investment more accessible for those with limited means.

In summary, rental property management is a crucial component of any real estate investment strategy. By understanding the principles and best practices of property management, individuals from low-income backgrounds can maximize their returns on investment and achieve financial independence. This subchapter will equip aspiring investors with the knowledge and tools they need to thrive in the world of real estate and pave their own path to prosperity.

Chapter 6: Building a Support Network for Success

Connecting with Mentors and Role Models

One of the most effective ways to break free from the cycle of poverty and achieve prosperity is by connecting with mentors and role models who have already walked the path to success. These individuals can provide invaluable guidance, support, and inspiration as you navigate your own journey from poverty to profits. In this subchapter, we will explore the importance of seeking out mentors and role models, and how their wisdom and experience can accelerate your personal and financial growth.

For anyone wanting to go from poverty to riches, finding the right mentors and role models is crucial. These individuals have already achieved the level of success you aspire to, and they can help you avoid common pitfalls and make smarter decisions. They can share their insights, offer practical advice, and provide a roadmap for your own success. By learning from those who have already achieved what you desire, you can significantly shorten your learning curve and increase your chances of achieving your goals.

In the niche of going from poverty to profits, mentors and role models who have successfully made the transition can offer specific strategies and advice tailored to your circumstances. They can help you identify opportunities, develop entrepreneurial skills, and navigate the challenges unique to individuals from disadvantaged backgrounds. By connecting with these mentors, you can gain the knowledge and confidence needed to start and grow your own profitable business.

Personal finance for low-income individuals is another niche where mentors and role models can make a profound impact. They can teach you the principles of budgeting, saving, and investing, providing you with the tools necessary to effectively manage your money and build wealth. By learning from those who have successfully managed their finances despite limited resources, you can develop the financial discipline and mindset needed to escape poverty and achieve financial independence.

Furthermore, mentors and role models in the realm of investing and real estate can open your eyes to the possibilities that exist for low-income earners. They can introduce you to investment opportunities that have the potential to generate substantial returns, even with limited capital. By following their guidance, you can learn how to leverage your resources and make informed investment decisions that can significantly improve your financial situation.

In conclusion, connecting with mentors and role models is a crucial step for anyone wanting to go from poverty to riches. These individuals can provide the wisdom, guidance, and inspiration necessary to accelerate your personal and financial growth. Whether you are interested in entrepreneurship, personal finance, investing, or real estate, seeking out mentors and role models who have already achieved success in these areas can be a game-changer. Their experiences and knowledge can help you avoid costly mistakes and achieve prosperity faster than you ever thought possible.

Joining Entrepreneurial and Investment Communities

If you are someone who dreams of going from poverty to riches, one of the most effective paths to prosperity is joining entrepreneurial and investment communities. These communities provide invaluable resources, support, and opportunities for individuals looking to escape poverty and build a successful future. In this subchapter, we will explore the benefits of joining these communities and how they can help you on your journey from poverty to profits.

Entrepreneurial communities are networks of like-minded individuals who share a passion for business and innovation. By joining these communities, you gain access to a wealth of knowledge and expertise from experienced entrepreneurs who have already achieved success. They can provide mentorship, guidance, and valuable insights that can help you avoid common pitfalls and accelerate your entrepreneurial journey.

Investment communities, on the other hand, focus on the world of finance and investing. These communities bring together individuals who are looking to grow their wealth through various investment opportunities. By joining these communities, you can learn about different investment strategies, gain access to exclusive investment opportunities, and connect with seasoned investors who can help you make informed decisions.

For low-income individuals, personal finance can be a significant challenge. However, by joining entrepreneurial and investment communities, you can gain the knowledge and skills needed to improve your financial situation. These communities often offer workshops, seminars, and training sessions on topics such as budgeting, saving, and debt management. By learning these essential personal finance skills, you can take control of your finances and start building a solid foundation for wealth creation.

Entrepreneurship is often seen as a privilege reserved for those with access to resources and networks. However, entrepreneurial communities specifically cater to individuals from disadvantaged backgrounds. They provide resources such as microloans, business development programs, and networking opportunities tailored to the unique challenges faced by low-income entrepreneurs.

Investment communities also offer opportunities for low-income individuals to enter the world of investing. Real estate investment, in particular, can be a lucrative avenue for low-income earners. Many investment communities focus on real estate investment opportunities, providing education on real estate investing and connecting individuals with affordable properties that can generate passive income.

In conclusion, joining entrepreneurial and investment communities is a crucial step for anyone wanting to go from poverty to riches. These communities offer a wealth of resources, support, and opportunities for personal finance management, entrepreneurship, and investing. By becoming a part of these communities, you can gain the knowledge, skills, and connections needed to transform your financial situation and achieve long-term prosperity.

Utilizing Government and Non-Profit Resources

When it comes to breaking free from the clutches of poverty and achieving financial prosperity, it's crucial to tap into all available resources. Thankfully, both the government and non-profit organizations offer a wide range of resources and assistance programs specifically designed to help individuals from disadvantaged backgrounds thrive. In this subchapter, we will explore how you can harness these resources to pave your path from poverty to profits.

One of the first steps in leveraging government resources is to become well-informed about the various programs available. From food assistance programs like SNAP (Supplemental Nutrition Assistance Program) to housing assistance like Section 8 vouchers, there are numerous avenues you can explore to alleviate your financial burdens. Understanding the eligibility criteria and application process for each program is essential. Additionally, don't hesitate to reach out to government agencies or local community centers for guidance and support in navigating these programs.

Non-profit organizations also play a pivotal role in providing assistance and resources to individuals looking to escape poverty. These organizations offer a plethora of services, ranging from financial education and job training programs to micro-loans and mentorship opportunities. Take the time to research and connect with non-profit organizations in your community that align with your goals and aspirations. They can provide valuable insights, support, and even funding to kickstart your journey towards entrepreneurship, personal finance management, or real estate investments.

Entrepreneurship can be a powerful tool for individuals from disadvantaged backgrounds to create wealth and achieve financial independence. Many non-profit organizations offer entrepreneurship programs and workshops that provide training, mentorship, and access to capital. These programs can equip you with the knowledge and skills needed to start and manage your own business. Additionally, government agencies often have initiatives in place to support small business owners, including grants, loans, and tax incentives. By tapping into these resources, you can turn your entrepreneurial dreams into reality.

Investing in real estate can also be a lucrative avenue for low-income earners to build wealth. Government programs like the Federal Housing Administration (FHA) loans can assist you in becoming a homeowner, even with a low credit score. Additionally, non-profit organizations may offer programs that provide financial assistance or educational resources for real estate investments. Exploring these opportunities can potentially open doors to passive income and long-term financial stability.

In conclusion, utilizing government and non-profit resources can significantly accelerate your journey from poverty to profits. By familiarizing yourself with the available programs and organizations, seeking guidance, and taking advantage of the support and opportunities they provide, you can lay a solid foundation for your financial success. Remember, you are not alone on this path. Reach out, embrace the resources available to you, and pave your way to prosperity.

Overcoming Stigma: Navigating Social Challenges

In the journey from poverty to profits, one of the most significant hurdles that individuals from disadvantaged backgrounds face is the stigma associated with their circumstances. Society often attaches negative stereotypes and biases to those who come from poverty, making it challenging to break free from the cycle of poverty and achieve financial prosperity. In this subchapter, we will explore the various social challenges individuals face and provide strategies to overcome stigma on the path to success.

The first step in overcoming stigma is to change our mindset. We must understand that our circumstances do not define us. Poverty is not a reflection of our worth or potential. By adopting a growth mindset and believing in our capabilities, we can break free from the limitations society places upon us.

Education and skill development are powerful tools to combat stigma. By investing in our personal development through acquiring knowledge and skills, we can enhance our self-confidence and prove our abilities to society. Pursuing higher education, vocational training, or participating in entrepreneurship programs tailored for individuals from disadvantaged backgrounds can provide the necessary skills to thrive in the business world.

Networking and building a support system are crucial in navigating social challenges. Connecting with like-minded individuals who have successfully transitioned from poverty to profits can provide valuable guidance and motivation. Joining communities, attending networking events, or seeking mentorship opportunities can help us overcome the isolation and build a strong support network.

Transparency and authenticity are essential in challenging stereotypes. By openly sharing our stories and experiences, we can break down barriers and inspire others. Embracing vulnerability and sharing our journey from poverty to profits can not only help us connect with others but also challenge societal perceptions.

Lastly, it is vital to remember that success is not solely measured by financial wealth. Contributing positively to our communities and helping others on their path to prosperity can be equally rewarding. By giving back and uplifting others, we can reshape the narrative surrounding poverty and redefine success on our own terms.

In conclusion, overcoming stigma is a critical aspect of the journey from poverty to profits. By shifting our mindset, investing in education and skills, building a support system, being transparent, and redefining success, we can navigate social challenges and break free from the limitations imposed upon us. Let us embrace our potential, challenge societal biases, and pave our own path to prosperity.

Chapter 7: Overcoming Obstacles and Staying Motivated

Dealing with setbacks: Turning Failures into Learning Opportunities

Failure is an inevitable part of the journey from poverty to profits. It is easy to become disheartened and discouraged when faced with setbacks, but it is important to remember that failure is not the end. In fact, setbacks can be valuable learning opportunities that propel us forward on the path to prosperity.

For anyone wanting to go from poverty to riches, it is crucial to develop resilience and a growth mindset. Rather than viewing failures as insurmountable obstacles, successful individuals see them as stepping stones to success. They understand that setbacks provide valuable insights and lessons that can be applied to future endeavors.

In the subchapter "Dealing with setbacks: Turning Failures into Learning Opportunities," we explore strategies and mindset shifts that can help individuals overcome setbacks and transform them into opportunities for growth. We delve into various niches that are particularly relevant to those seeking to escape poverty and build wealth, including personal finance, entrepreneurship, investing, and real estate.

One key aspect of dealing with setbacks is reframing failure. Instead of viewing it as a personal reflection of incompetence or inadequacy, we encourage readers to embrace a growth mindset that sees failure as a natural part of the learning process. By reframing failure as a stepping stone towards success, individuals can bounce back from setbacks with renewed determination and resilience.

Another important aspect we discuss is the importance of learning from failures. We provide practical strategies for analyzing setbacks and extracting valuable lessons from them. By identifying what went wrong and why, individuals can adjust their strategies, refine their approach, and increase their chances of success in future endeavors.

Additionally, we explore the concept of resilience and how it can be cultivated. We provide practical tips and techniques for bouncing back from setbacks, including building a strong support network, practicing self-care, and developing a positive mindset.

Ultimately, setbacks are not the end of the road but rather opportunities for growth and learning. By embracing failures as stepping stones on the path to prosperity, individuals can develop the resilience and mindset necessary to overcome obstacles and achieve their goals. In this subchapter, readers will gain valuable insights and practical strategies for navigating setbacks and transforming them into opportunities for success.

Overcoming Imposter Syndrome: Believing in Your Abilities

In the pursuit of prosperity, one of the biggest obstacles that many individuals face is the Imposter Syndrome. This nagging feeling of inadequacy and self-doubt can be especially prevalent among those who have experienced poverty or come from disadvantaged backgrounds. However, it is crucial to recognize that your background does not define your potential for success. In this subchapter, we will explore how to overcome Imposter Syndrome and start believing in your abilities, regardless of your past circumstances.

Imposter Syndrome often stems from comparing ourselves to others and feeling like we don't belong in certain spaces or industries. However, it's important to remember that success comes in many different forms, and everyone's journey is unique. By recognizing your own strengths, skills, and experiences, you can begin to build confidence in your abilities.

One effective strategy to overcome Imposter Syndrome is to focus on your accomplishments. Take the time to reflect on the challenges you have overcome and the progress you have made. Celebrate your small wins and use them as evidence of your competence. Additionally, surround yourself with a supportive network of individuals who believe in your potential. Seek out mentors or join communities that can provide guidance and encouragement on your path to prosperity.

Another way to combat Imposter Syndrome is through continuous learning and skill development. Invest in your personal finance education, entrepreneurship skills, or real estate investment knowledge. By acquiring new knowledge and honing your expertise, you can become more confident in your abilities and prove to yourself that you are capable of achieving financial success.

It is also important to shift your mindset from a fear of failure to a growth mindset. Embrace challenges as opportunities for growth and view setbacks as valuable learning experiences. Understand that making mistakes is a natural part of the journey to prosperity and that it does not define your worth or potential.

Believing in your abilities is crucial for taking the leap into entrepreneurship or making strategic investments. By overcoming Imposter Syndrome, you can unlock your full potential and tap into the opportunities that will lead you from poverty to profits. Remember, your past does not determine your future, and with the right mindset and belief in yourself, you can achieve financial independence and prosperity.

Maintaining Self-Care and Wellness for Long-Term Success

In the pursuit of transforming one's life from poverty to prosperity, it is crucial to recognize the importance of maintaining self-care and wellness. The journey from poverty to profits can be demanding and challenging, both physically and mentally. Therefore, it is essential to prioritize self-care practices to ensure long-term success and overall well-being.

First and foremost, taking care of your physical health is paramount. Engaging in regular exercise, eating a balanced diet, and getting enough restorative sleep are fundamental aspects of self-care. Regular exercise not only improves physical health but also boosts mental clarity and provides an outlet for stress relief. A nutritious diet fuels your body and mind, enabling you to maintain high levels of energy and focus throughout your journey. Adequate sleep is crucial for rejuvenation and maintaining optimal cognitive function, allowing you to make sound decisions and stay focused on your goals.

Equally important is nurturing your mental and emotional well-being. The path from poverty to profits can be emotionally taxing, and it is vital to prioritize mental health to prevent burnout and maintain resilience. Practicing mindfulness, meditation, or any form of relaxation techniques can help alleviate stress, improve concentration, and enhance overall mental well-being. Additionally, seeking support from friends, family, or professionals can provide valuable guidance and help you navigate the challenges along the way.

Entrepreneurship and investing require continuous learning and growth. Therefore, it is essential to cultivate a lifelong learning mindset. Investing in personal development, such as attending workshops, seminars, or reading books related to your niche, can help expand your knowledge and skills, ultimately contributing to your long-term success. Additionally, surrounding yourself with like-minded individuals through networking events or joining supportive communities can provide valuable insights, encouragement, and accountability.

As you progress on your journey, it is crucial to strike a balance between work and personal life. While a strong work ethic is essential, neglecting your personal life can lead to burnout and hinder your long-term success. Carve out time for hobbies, relaxation, and spending quality time with loved ones. Remember that achieving prosperity is not solely about financial gains but also about creating a fulfilling and balanced life.

In conclusion, maintaining self-care and wellness is a critical component of long-term success when transitioning from poverty to profits. Prioritizing physical health, nurturing mental and emotional well-being, investing in personal development, and striking a balance between work and personal life are essential ingredients for achieving prosperity. By integrating these self-care practices into your journey, you will not only enhance your chances of financial success but also cultivate a fulfilling and meaningful life. Remember, taking care of yourself is not a luxury but a necessity on the path to prosperity.

Celebrating Milestones: Recognizing and Appreciating Progress

In our journey towards prosperity, it is crucial to acknowledge and celebrate the milestones we achieve along the way. Recognizing and appreciating progress is not only a source of motivation but also a reminder of how far we have come from poverty to profits. This subchapter explores the significance of celebrating milestones and offers valuable insights for anyone wanting to transform their lives and escape the clutches of poverty.

For those on the path from poverty to profits, acknowledging milestones is a key aspect of personal finance for low-income individuals. By setting achievable goals and celebrating each small victory, we cultivate a positive mindset and create a foundation for financial success. Whether it's paying off a debt, saving a certain amount, or starting a side business, every milestone is a step towards financial independence.

Entrepreneurship holds immense potential for individuals from disadvantaged backgrounds to break free from poverty. By embracing entrepreneurship, we can create our own opportunities and redefine our financial destiny. This subchapter emphasizes the importance of celebrating entrepreneurial milestones, such as launching a business, securing a significant client, or achieving a certain revenue target. These milestones not only validate our efforts but also encourage us to push further and grow our ventures.

Investing wisely is another crucial aspect of escaping poverty and building wealth. For individuals looking to escape poverty through investments, celebrating milestones becomes a way to track progress and stay motivated. Each milestone in the investment journey, whether it's reaching a specific savings goal or achieving a positive return on investment, brings us closer to financial freedom. Recognizing these milestones helps us stay focused on our investment strategy and inspires us to continue making sound financial decisions.

Real estate investment presents an excellent opportunity for low-income earners to build wealth and secure a better future. This subchapter explores the importance of celebrating milestones in real estate investment, such as purchasing the first property, successfully renting it out, or achieving a certain level of rental income. These milestones not only validate our efforts but also inspire confidence in the potential of real estate as a pathway to prosperity.

In conclusion, celebrating milestones is a vital aspect of going from poverty to profits. By recognizing and appreciating progress, we reinforce our commitment to financial success. Whether it's personal finance, entrepreneurship, investing, or real estate, each milestone brings us closer to our goals and motivates us to keep pushing forward. Let us celebrate every step of the way and embrace the journey towards prosperity.

Chapter 8: Taking Action and Achieving Prosperity

Developing a Step-by-Step Action Plan

In order to embark on a journey towards prosperity, it is essential to have a well-defined action plan that will guide you through the process. This subchapter will outline the necessary steps to develop a comprehensive action plan, tailored specifically for individuals aspiring to go from poverty to riches. Whether you are looking to improve your personal finances, start your own business, invest wisely, or explore real estate opportunities, this chapter will provide you with practical advice on how to get started.

Step 1: Set Clear Goals
The first step towards prosperity is to define your goals. What does success mean to you? Is it achieving financial stability, starting your own business, or acquiring real estate assets? By setting clear and tangible goals, you will have a target to work towards and stay motivated throughout your journey.

Step 2: Assess Your Current Situation
Conduct a thorough assessment of your current financial status and skills. Identify your strengths and weaknesses, as well as any obstacles that may hinder your progress. This self-evaluation will serve as a foundation for creating a plan that is realistic and achievable.

Step 3: Educate Yourself
Knowledge is power, especially when it comes to personal finance, entrepreneurship, investing, and real estate. Take advantage of educational resources, both online and offline, to enhance your understanding in these areas. Attend seminars, read books, listen to podcasts, and seek mentorship from experts in your chosen niche.

Step 4: Create a Budget and Savings Plan
Developing a budget is crucial for managing your finances effectively. Determine your income, expenses, and savings goals, and allocate your money accordingly. Create a savings plan that will allow you to build an emergency fund and invest in opportunities that will lead you towards prosperity.

Step 5: Start Small and Take Action
Don't wait for the perfect moment to start. Begin small by taking actionable steps towards your goals. Whether it's saving a portion of your income, starting a side business, or investing in low-risk opportunities, every small step counts. Remember, consistency is key.

Step 6: Seek Support and Networking Opportunities
Surround yourself with like-minded individuals who share your aspirations. Join local community groups, attend networking events, and engage with individuals who have successfully gone from poverty to profits. Their experiences and advice can provide valuable insights and support along your journey.

Step 7: Review and Adjust Your Plan
Regularly review your action plan, reassess your goals, and make necessary adjustments. As you progress, you may encounter new opportunities or face unexpected challenges. Flexibility and adaptability are crucial for long-term success.

By following these steps and developing a step-by-step action plan, you will be well on your way to transforming your life from poverty to prosperity. Remember, the path to riches is not without its challenges, but with determination, perseverance, and a well-structured action plan, you can achieve the financial freedom you desire.

Putting Your Financial Knowledge into Practice

Now that you have gained a solid understanding of financial concepts and strategies, it's time to put that knowledge into practice. In this subchapter, we will explore practical ways to apply your financial knowledge in order to transition from poverty to riches.

Going from Poverty to Profits:
One of the first steps towards financial prosperity is to establish a solid foundation. Start by creating a budget that reflects your income and expenses, and make a commitment to live within your means. Set realistic financial goals and develop a plan to achieve them. This may include finding ways to increase your income through side businesses or freelancing, and reducing unnecessary expenses.

Personal Finance for Low-Income Individuals: Low-income individuals often face unique challenges when it comes to personal finance. However, with the right strategies, it is possible to build wealth even on a limited income. This subchapter will provide practical tips for budgeting, saving, and managing debt effectively. It will also explore government assistance programs and other resources that can help individuals maximize their financial potential.

Entrepreneurship for Individuals from Disadvantaged Backgrounds: Entrepreneurship can be a powerful tool for individuals from disadvantaged backgrounds to escape poverty and build wealth. This section will explore the key steps to starting a successful business, including identifying opportunities, developing a business plan, and securing funding. It will also address the specific challenges faced by entrepreneurs from low-income backgrounds and provide guidance on overcoming them.

Investing for Individuals Looking to Escape Poverty:
Investing can be a powerful wealth-building tool, but it can also be intimidating, especially for those with limited financial resources. This subchapter will demystify the world of investing and provide practical guidance on how to get started. It will cover different investment options, such as stocks, bonds, mutual funds, and real estate, and provide strategies for minimizing risk and maximizing returns.

Real Estate Investment Opportunities for Low-Income Earners:
Real estate can offer a unique opportunity for low-income earners to build wealth. This section will explore the various ways individuals can get involved in real estate investing, including buying rental properties, investing in real estate investment trusts (REITs), or participating in crowdfunding platforms. It will also address the potential challenges and provide tips for success in this area.

By putting your financial knowledge into practice, you can start your journey towards prosperity. Whether it's through budgeting, entrepreneurship, investing, or real estate, the strategies and tips in this subchapter will empower you to take control of your financial future and turn your dreams of escaping poverty into a reality.

Tracking and Evaluating Your Progress

In your journey from poverty to profits, it is crucial to continuously track and evaluate your progress. By doing so, you will gain valuable insights into your financial situation and make informed decisions that will propel you towards success. This subchapter will guide you through the process of effectively tracking and evaluating your progress, ensuring that you stay on the path to prosperity.

First and foremost, it is essential to establish clear goals. Define what success means to you and set specific, measurable, achievable, relevant, and time-bound (SMART) goals. Whether it is saving a certain amount of money, starting your own business, or investing in real estate, having well-defined objectives will serve as a compass throughout your journey.

Once you have established your goals, it's time to track your progress. Start by creating a budget that outlines your income, expenses, and savings. This will help you understand where your money is coming from, where it is going, and how much you are saving. Utilize various financial tracking tools and apps that are specifically designed for low-income individuals, as they can simplify the process and provide valuable insights into your financial habits.

Regularly review your budget and compare your actual income and expenses against your planned budget. This will enable you to identify any areas where you may be overspending or opportunities to increase your savings. Additionally, consider tracking your net worth, which is the difference between your assets and liabilities. As you progress towards prosperity, your net worth should increase over time.

Evaluation is equally important in tracking your progress. Reflect on your achievements and challenges regularly. Celebrate your successes, no matter how small, as they will motivate you to keep going. Identify any obstacles or setbacks that you have encountered and brainstorm strategies to overcome them. Seek feedback from trusted mentors or advisors who can provide objective insights and help you make necessary adjustments.

Remember that tracking and evaluating your progress is a continuous process. As you reach your goals and set new ones, make sure to update your tracking methods accordingly. By doing so, you will have a comprehensive overview of your financial journey and be better equipped to make informed decisions that will propel you towards prosperity.

In conclusion, tracking and evaluating your progress is vital for anyone wanting to go from poverty to riches. By setting clear goals, tracking your finances, and regularly evaluating your progress, you will gain valuable insights into your financial situation and make informed decisions that will lead you to success. Stay committed to the process, celebrate your achievements, and learn from your setbacks. With dedication and perseverance, you can transform your life and achieve financial prosperity.

Celebrating and Sharing Your Success Stories

In the journey from poverty to profits, it is essential to celebrate and share your success stories. This subchapter will delve into the importance of recognizing and sharing your accomplishments, as well as the benefits it brings to individuals looking to go from poverty to riches.

When you achieve success, whether it be a small milestone or a significant breakthrough, it is crucial to take a moment to celebrate. Celebrating your successes provides a boost of motivation and reinforces your belief in your ability to overcome challenges. It allows you to acknowledge the progress you have made and the hard work you have put in to reach your goals. By celebrating your success, you cultivate a positive mindset and build confidence in your abilities.

Equally important is sharing your success stories. By sharing your journey from poverty to profits, you inspire others who are on a similar path. Your story serves as a powerful reminder that it is possible to overcome adversity and create a life of abundance. Sharing your experiences can also provide guidance and practical tips for those who are looking to improve their personal finance, start their own businesses, invest wisely, or explore real estate opportunities.

For individuals from disadvantaged backgrounds, celebrating and sharing success stories can be a game-changer. It helps break the cycle of poverty by providing tangible examples of individuals who have overcome similar challenges. By showcasing success stories, this subchapter aims to inspire and motivate individuals to take action, step out of their comfort zone, and pursue their dreams of financial independence.

Furthermore, celebrating and sharing success stories within the niches of personal finance, entrepreneurship, investing, and real estate investment opportunities is particularly beneficial. These niches offer practical strategies and resources for low-income earners, providing them with the tools they need to escape poverty and achieve prosperity. By highlighting success stories within these niches, individuals can gain valuable insights into the specific steps they can take to improve their financial situation.

In conclusion, celebrating and sharing your success stories is a crucial aspect of the journey from poverty to profits. By recognizing and sharing your accomplishments, you inspire others who are looking to escape poverty and achieve financial independence. This subchapter aims to encourage individuals from various backgrounds to celebrate their successes and share their stories, thereby creating a community of support and motivation in the pursuit of prosperity.

Conclusion: Embracing the Journey to Prosperity

Congratulations! You have taken the first step towards transforming your life and embracing the journey to prosperity. Throughout this book, "The Path to Prosperity: From Poverty to Profits," we have explored various strategies and insights that can help anyone wanting to go from poverty to riches. Whether you are interested in going from poverty to profits, managing personal finance, entrepreneurship, investing, or real estate opportunities, this book has provided you with the tools and knowledge to start your journey towards financial freedom.

Going from Poverty to Profits is not an easy task, but it is possible with determination, hard work, and the right mindset. It all begins with a strong desire to change your current circumstances and a willingness to take action. Remember, your past does not define your future. Embrace the belief that you have the power to create a better life for yourself and your loved ones.

One crucial aspect of this journey is personal finance. We have discussed the importance of budgeting, saving, and investing wisely, even with a limited income. By understanding and implementing sound financial principles, you can gradually build wealth and escape the cycle of poverty. It is essential to educate yourself about financial literacy and seek opportunities to improve your financial knowledge continuously.

Entrepreneurship can be a game-changer for individuals from disadvantaged backgrounds. By harnessing your unique skills, talents, and passions, you can create your own business and be in control of your financial destiny. We have explored various strategies to start and grow a successful business, including market research, business planning, marketing, and financial management. Remember, entrepreneurship requires dedication, perseverance, and a willingness to adapt to changing circumstances.

Investing is another powerful tool to escape poverty and build wealth. We have discussed different investment options, including stocks, bonds, mutual funds, and real estate. By learning the basics of investing and developing a long-term investment plan, you can make your money work for you and achieve financial independence.

Real estate investment opportunities are particularly appealing for low-income earners. We have explored creative ways to enter the real estate market, such as house hacking, real estate crowdfunding, and government programs. Real estate can provide a steady stream of income and long-term wealth if approached with careful research and planning.

In conclusion, the journey from poverty to prosperity is within your reach. By embracing the strategies and insights shared in this book, you can transform your life and achieve financial success. Remember, it won't happen overnight, but with persistence, dedication, and the right mindset, you can overcome any obstacles and create a better future for yourself and your loved ones. Start today and embrace the journey to prosperity. You deserve it!

Appendix: Additional Resources and Tools for Financial Success

Congratulations on taking the first step towards transforming your financial future! In this appendix, we have compiled a comprehensive list of additional resources and tools to help you navigate the path from poverty to profits. Whether you are looking to improve your personal finance, start your own business, invest wisely, or explore real estate opportunities, this guide is tailored to meet your specific needs.

1. Going from Poverty to Profits:
- "The Path to Prosperity Workbook": A companion workbook to the main book, providing practical exercises and strategies to implement the principles discussed.
- Online Forums and Support Groups: Connect with like-minded individuals who are also on their journey to financial success. Share experiences, seek advice, and find inspiration from those who have already made the transition.

2. Personal Finance for Low-Income Individuals:
- Budgeting Tools and Apps: Utilize user-friendly budgeting tools and mobile apps to manage your income and expenses effectively. Some popular options include Mint, YNAB, and PocketGuard.
- Credit Building Resources: Access free resources that guide you on building and repairing your credit score, such as the Consumer Financial Protection Bureau's website and Credit Karma.

3. Entrepreneurship for Individuals from Disadvantaged Backgrounds:
- Small Business Administration (SBA) Programs: Explore SBA resources like online courses, mentorship programs, and business planning tools to help you start and grow your own business.
- Microfinance Institutions: Discover organizations that offer small loans and business development support specifically designed for individuals from disadvantaged backgrounds.

4. Investing for Individuals Looking to Escape Poverty:
- Online Investment Platforms: Explore reputable online investment platforms, such as Acorns or Robinhood, that allow you to start investing with small amounts of money.
- Investment Education: Access free online investment courses, podcasts, and blogs to develop your knowledge and understanding of various investment opportunities.

5. Real Estate Investment Opportunities for Low-Income Earners:
- HUD Resources: The U.S. Department of Housing and Urban Development provides resources on affordable housing, rental assistance programs, and homeownership opportunities.
- Real Estate Investment Books: Read books like "The ABCs of Real Estate Investing" by Ken McElroy or "The Book on Rental Property Investing" by Brandon Turner to gain insights into real estate investment strategies.

Remember, the journey from poverty to profits requires dedication, persistence, and continuous learning. Use these additional resources and tools to empower yourself and take control of your financial future. With the right knowledge and support, you can overcome obstacles and achieve the prosperity you deserve. Good luck on your path to financial success!

The Path to Prosperity: from Poverty to Profits

Poverty is a complex issue that affects millions of individuals around the world. In this subchapter, we will delve into the definition and causes of poverty, providing valuable insights for anyone wanting to go from poverty to riches.

www.ingramcontent.com/pod-product-compliance
Lightning Source LLC
La Vergne TN
LVHW022109200926
848481LV00003B/1122

* 9 7 9 8 2 2 3 9 7 1 6 6 5 *